STOCKHOLM HORIZONS

by Jeppe Wikström

Bokförlaget Max Ström

© Bokförlaget Max Ström 2007
Text and photos: Jeppe Wikström
Photo assistant: Erik G. Svensson
Translation: Kim Loughran with Ariane Sains
Design: Patric Leo
Layout: Petra Ahston Inkapööl
Repro: Fälth & Hässler, Värnamo, Sweden
Printing: Imago, Singapore 2007

ISBN 978-91-89204-63-8

CONTENTS

The bells above me are pealing five as I open the door and stand to gaze at the city below me. My eyes strain to get used to the dark. At first there's little more than a jumble of lights, lines and shapes – a gigantic city board game. But there's no disorientation; I know the view far too well for that.

I'm on the City Hall tower viewing platform, with the panorama of the city below. I've slept the night here. The parliament buildings, the royal palace, the five boxy office blocks in the central business district, the Grand Hôtel – all are etched against the blush of early sunrise. For morning exercise, I stroll around, counting the church towers within sight. I make it 25. The most easily recognisable are the redbrick steeples of Klara and Johannes and the city's only twin-spire at Högalid. The lighted clock dial in Klara's tower shines on me like an eye, but all other lights are down and windows shut.

The city slumbers.

It's a still morning and the faint, dawn start-up of the city is clearly audible up here in the tower. On the street just below me, a newspaper deliverer tows his trolley by, its unoiled wheels nagging. He's on his slow way home. And in a schooner alongside the quay, a pump hums in regular spasms.

The first of the exploratory morning traffic can be sensed and the infrequent cars on the main urban approach artery buzz as though rudely awakened. Suddenly a siren is switched on and an ambulance, blue light pulsing, accelerates along the south side of Riddarfjärden's quiet waters. It speeds towards Västerbro Bridge and when it reaches the top of the arched bridge, its wail pours out across the entire city. From the Central Station, electronic blips frame a voice announcing the day's first departures.

In the growing light, I make out a couple seated on a bench in the Old Town. It looks at first as though they are sleeping in tight embrace, but using a telephoto lens I see that they are lost in an endless kiss. More lights are flicked on in offices and homes and on the heights of the South Mount, bedclothes are being shaken from a window.

Slowly, majestically, a glowing sphere floats free from the horizon. Turning around I see that the dome of Kungsholmen Church is on fire. The communications tower at Kaknäs, the highest structure in the city, is sending out vivid sunlight flashes from the observation deck windows. But down at street level, the city is still enveloped in grey. Shades of grey abound. Postal delivery trucks leaving their central depot haven't yet changed into their usual yellow and the shadowy figures flitting by near the Central Station could all be air hostesses in regulation dark blue. But up on Kungsholmen Island, the high-rises are bathed in red sunlight; a man on a balcony, smoking a cigarette, protects his pained eyes with a free hand.

High above the old shantytown-turned-champagne town, Östermalm, a hot-air balloon drifts languidly.

After a while, the commuter and metro trains become more frequent and a freight train leaves for the south. It's a long one, so long that the locomotive has passed the Old Town before the last wagons have left the Central Station. Fascinated, I count 43 of them while the train's steely rhythm echoes like a heartbeat in the early morning. An archipelago ferry appears, on its way in to a downtown quay. It may be my imagination, but it's bringing with it a soft easterly breeze, smelling faintly of seaweed.

Down by the Södermalm traffic terminus, commuter buses are wheeling in. Above the bus station, a man or woman is looking into rubbish containers for cans and bottles, dreaming of deposit money. A small lake ferry casts off from below the terminus with the day's first passengers. I follow its route, and as it passes the last of the inner city boatyards I notice that the working day has already begun; a small steel boat of indeterminate type is being winched up the slipway.

Street traffic is now in full flow. On the Söderleden freeway, vehicles progress slowly northwards, into the city. But on the freeway skirting the waterway behind the Central Station, the day's first gridlock is not far off. Suddenly: tyre screech, sheet metal against sheet metal, glass tinkling on asphalt. The three cars apparently involved have brought traffic to almost complete standstill. Three drivers are all out of their cars, flapping an irate semaphore with their arms. It takes about ten minutes for a police car and two tow trucks to reach the scene.

Out in the saltwater harbour, a cruise liner is mooring, helped by a tug. Its huge white bulk is not yet at the quayside before the bustling Finland ferry, the *Mariella*, accelerates past Beckholmen Islet, heading for the open Baltic. The tug's propellers labour to turn the liner's colossal body in the tight space allotted, attracting a large number of white feathers. The feathers' owners gratefully dive for fish in the churning water.

On the raised concrete legs of the third major freeway, sunlight glints from the windscreens of the countless vehicles crossing Lake Mälaren. A motorboat leaves a small marina. Two men on board the school ship *Polhem* are lowering a lifeboat while, further on, two kayaks snake out from shore, leaving scarcely any wake behind.

By the Grand Hôtel, the arm of a giant crane swings back and forth, and a scaffold is removed. Way over to the northwest, a helicopter is lifting something onto the roof of the Wenner-Gren Center, probably yet another mobile telephony relay station.

The sun is warming now. Sunrays play in the swirling waters of the channel by the Old Town. Sounds have already become impossible to separate; the city delivers a fused hum. At the quay in front of the Grand Hôtel, an archipelago ferry backs out from its berth but I can no longer make out its whistle. I can, however, hear sirens somewhere west in the city; it could be engines from the fire station by Fridhemsplan. I start looking for the fire but find no pillar of smoke anywhere. The bells above my head ring nine and as I look toward the royal palace, I see the flag being raised.

What makes a city? Many might say large buildings and things to marvel at, others would answer factories and business districts. But this must be subordinate to what happens in a city and to the people that live there. A city is principally a forum for mankind's countless activities. We live, think, work, buy, sell, study, love, enjoy and suffer in the city. Because of all these, we and our ancestors created a structure – the framework that is the city.

While still small, a city will tolerate control. When it grows, things start to happen independently. The accumulation of its history gives the city a breath equivalent to all the people who live and work in it. The city becomes an organism.

This is true of all large cities. But this isn't just any city. This one, built on hard bedrock and surrounded by forest where a lake system meets the sea, is the city where I live. Me and a million others.

My horizon, Stockholm.

GAMLA STAN

Gamla Stan, the Old Town, is just that: old, narrow alleys and noble buildings — both village and relic of Sweden's days of military greatness. Here, executions have wet cobblestones with blood, triumphant kings have paraded and immortal poets have sung — and caroused. These alleys breathe history.

This is where Stockholm began. On this little islet, no wider than 500 metres, right where Lake Mälaren mixes water with the brackish Baltic Sea. The people that populated this region established a community here at the end of the 12th century to control shipping and protect the prosperous villages around the lake. The islet quickly became an important market centre. Sometime in the 13th century, it began to be known as Stockholm – literally: log islet – probably because of its extensive wooden ramparts. By the end of the century, the cluster of small houses, protected by fortress and cathedral, was no longer identifiable as a fishing village. The city was nascent.

Dramatic centuries followed. The town grew amid battles and bloodshed. Gustav Vasa rode in on his mission to unite Sweden. Stockholm lost its independence but became the capital of the kingdom. The town grew even larger. Sweden became a Great Power with half of northern Europe governed from Stockholm. The town continued to grow, even more rapidly, doubling its population in the 17th century. Fires and plagues were visited on the town, kings were crowned and kings buried. Royal balls were held and peasants marched, torches on high.

The Old Town breathes history but is no dusty museum. The alleys are crammed with shops and galleries. Restaurants make use of the old vaulted cellars to serve their guests and buildings dating back to the 16th century house both offices and homes. Cathedral services have been held since the 13th century; there has been a guard detail at the palace or its predecessor since 1523; and there's a tobacconist on Stora Nygatan Street where smokes have been sold since 1859. Stockholmers stroll by on the cobblestones, their footsteps echoing through the alleys. The smallest sound is magnified: a radio, a gurgling child or kitchen noises can be heard far down the lane.

Little more than a century ago, there were plans afoot to demolish almost all of the Old Town. Much had become slum. But there were vociferous protests from cultural icons such as playwright-poet-author August Strindberg and the cherished painter Carl Larsson. Decades of inquiries followed until a city plan was agreed on in 1965. It called for renewal through renovation rather than removal of buildings and today, almost all of the Old Town's buildings fall under the law of preservation of historical buildings. These properties are now lovingly maintained and the area is in good shape, with many of its traditions intact.

The Old Town is actually four islands. The smallest has only one building. The next largest has the parliament house, Riksdagshuset, and a unique Medieval Museum. The third, Riddarholmen, has a church, government offices and law courts. Apart from Riddarholmen, where a single family lives, the only island that has homes is the largest, Stadsholmen. In the evenings, the silence from the empty streets and squares of Riddarholmen contrasts with the

bustle on the adjoining island. The main reason is that the two are separated by a whining motorway, a gash in the very heart of the city.

Most people you meet in the Old Town live elsewhere; they're either tourists or Stockholmers from other areas employed here or just rubbernecking. There are a great many offices in the Old Town; more people lived here in the 14th century than today – now there are no more than three thousand registered residents. It is not an easy place to live; at the height of the summer tourist season, the main street can be a nightmare for residents. Threading your way home through hordes of tourists and street musicans can be ... vexing. Transporting anything by car to an Old Town address is also extremely tricky – and don't even dream of parking! Apartments tend to be cramped and dark, with small rooms and low ceilings. Daylight has to wrestle its way into the narrow alleyways.

No matter; the people who live here wouldn't dream of moving. They love the small town atmosphere and the sense of living in historical surroundings. Besides, the Old Town is surrounded by, and in easy reach of, the other inner-city areas. And the oldest marketplace, Kornhamnstorg, is counted as the city's true geographic centre.

Gamla Stan is not only the birthplace of Stockholm; it's the nucleus.

Cobblestones on Brunnsgränd add to the city's folio of patterns (p. 10).

The Old Town's four islands are easily discernible from the air (p. 12–13).

The courtyards of the Old Town offer marvellous variety. This cramped courtyard presents only a glimpse of the sky (p. 14).

The street of Prästgatan used to be just inside the oldest of the city's walls. Time peels away here, telescoping us to the Middle Ages, helped by the absence of souvenir shops and plastic signs. Many buildings have golden-ochre facades from the 1700s, still typical for the Old Town (p. 17).

The apartments in the Old Town are often small and dark, so residents make inventive use of their roofs. Amidst a maze of ladders, a landing becomes a sun deck (p. 18).

Dawn over Skeppsbron, in the past a street of ships' brokers (pp. 20–21).

The relief guard marches across Högvakt's Terrace at the Royal Palace (right).

Anders Hellström, by day a building superintendent, by night a rock musician and fire-eater. Even fire-eaters need practice, and Anders seizes a few minutes before a paid performance to perfect his art (pp. 24–25).

There are many sides to the palace. When the royal family entertains officially, the building is a festival of light in darkness (pp. 26–27).

Henrik Björlin adjusts the minute hand on the cathedral clock. Stockholm's sole cathedral is believed to be 700 years old, although the 66-metre-high spire dates from 1743 (right).

From the cathedral tower, with the harbour to one side, the German Church spire centre-right and, beyond, Söder Mount (pp. 30–31).

SÖDERMALM

"Söder" sometimes feels very un-Swedish. Strewn among apartment blocks and scuffed streets are wooden cottages and secret gardens. Dramatic cliffs above the harbour electrify the landscape. Söder is jam-packed with pubs and people, with nobody putting on airs. Söder's reputation is for small-time crooks, earthiness, an inventive vocabulary, and good-neighbourliness. More is owed to myth than legend, but why spoil a good story?

Södermalm, the South Mount, is the only one of Stockholm's areas with the distinction of a nickname: "Söder". A map of Söder suggests a mouth, with the long slash of Ringvägen, the Ring Road, the smiling lips. The map will also tell you that Söder is the largest of all the inner city areas, almost five kilometres long and 7.4 square kilometres in area. A leisurely walk around the periphery, keeping the water always close by, will take almost four hours. In population as well, Söder is king: almost 100,000 people live here.

But size has little to do with Söder's famous charm; on the contrary, the charm is its small-town feel. Much has been made of Söder's famous working-class housing, which came to represent the best in Sweden's urban, blue-collar culture: folksiness, good-neighbourliness and a lust for life. Even though originally there was no deliberate conservationist policy maintaining them, there are still a couple of hundred buildings that could be described as typical Söder housing. They have survived because it was predominantly working-class. Söder was ignored by planners eager to use Sweden's growing prosperity to erect grander homes and buildings, razing the old almost indiscriminately. In the 1920s, however, the first deliberate steps were taken to preserve Söder's legendary buildings.

The small-town feel is accentuated by all the gardening allotments, tiny plots of land rented by the city to folks who want to grow flowers, vegetables or fruit – or simply rig up a hammock and pretend they're lazy country-folk.

Söder has always been a magnet for artists; there are far more artists' studios here than anywhere else in the city. It's also Stockholm's pub hub, where pub-crawling is at least easy on the shoe leather. This artsy, small-town aura notwithstanding, the area also includes some of the most densely packed housing estates, a sometimes rude contrast to their surroundings.

Söder has always been thought of as a working-class area. And from the streets of low-rent housing came strong local pride and a rich argot famous for its humour. All this led to a deeply rooted sense of belonging. In the words of Söder's famous writer, Per Anders Fogelström: "Söder is cheeky enough to make shame into glory and glory into shame. Old Söder hands still wear memories of childhood poverty as though they were medals."

The archetypal Söder male was known as a Söderkis. He was possessed of charm, friendliness, a smoth line of gab – and on a hot day could be partial to a drop of beer.

Today, little of the working-class ethic remains. The average income varies little from other areas and Söder has become trendy. Not everything has been erased: Söder's residents are still folksier and friendlier and more direct. Other Stockholmers may claim these same characteristics, but perhaps the very myth of its charm makes Söder resemble the myth more closely. Because the proverbial Söderkis is happy to shoot the bull with

anybody who comes his way, just being on Söder empowers anyone to do just that. And who stands to gain if Söder turns out to be no different than anywhere else?

The area has more restaurants and bars than any other part of Stockholm – or Sweden, come to think of it. There are more than a thousand places to eat, drink and be merry – roughly as many per head as there were in the aquavit-soaked days of the great minstrel poets of the 18th century. (With one exception: only a third of the bars and restaurants are fully licensed to serve spirits, including aquavit.)

Söder is Stockholm's biggest district vertically as well as in surface area and population. Testifying to the drama of Söder's topography is the large number of steps and stairs. There are no fewer than 271 public stairways linking streets of differing levels.

The highest point in the inner city is here, fully 54 metres above sea level. From the clifftop, you look down on the harbour and most of the city.

And the city looks back up at Söder.

Students at Götgatan (p. 32).

French Bay is mirror-calm in the summer dawn. The street of Hornsgatan, a main drag, cuts Söder in two (pp. 34–35).

On the commercial artery of Hornsgatan, motorists are spear carriers in a giant, afternoon shadow opera (p. 36).

The old wooden houses of Söder are clustered like villages in the landscape of the city. Some, like this one in Vita Bergen Park, could be mistaken for cottages in the woods of Sörmland province, south of the capital (p. 39).

Högalid's twin-spired church is unique in the city and a favourite landmark (p. 40).

As if possessed by movement, these 18th and 19th century buildings seem to clamber up the hill at Mariaberget, watched by regal dwellings on the crest (right).

Looking back towards the city, the old prison island of Långholmen on the left and the twin spires of Högalid Church atop Söder Island to the right, with the canal cutting through the trees straight ahead. The buildings in the foreground are from the 1940s (pp. 44–45).

The 1,361 coloured 25-watt lightbulbs on the city's oldest illuminated advertisement were first switched on in 1906. It's said that the flow of toothpaste onto the brush used to cause horses to rear. Twice a year, Björn Nyquist changes burned-out bulbs (pp. 46–47).

Neighbours share the season's first gooseberries at Tanto, Söder's biggest allotment colony (pp. 48–49).

The wading pond at Nytorget Square draws children from across Söder. In the background, the 78-metre-high spire of Sofia Church (left).

Summer green is all around. The redbrick serenity of Sofia Church rises from among the trees of Vita Bergen Park, a popular spot for outdoor performances on long summer evenings (pp. 52–53).

KUNGSHOLMEN

Stockholm is managed from Kungsholmen Island – most city authorities are headquartered here. But there's more: water, parks and vibrant street life. What Stockholmers used to know as a backwater has a sneaky charm. Trendsetters have moved in and the mean age of residents is dropping. There's a mundane side – gravel depots, ugly industrial sites, factories and newspaper offices – but Kungsholmen is also like your granny's attic: messy, exciting and filled with heirlooms.

Kungsholmen, King's Island, has the noblest name of all the capital's areas. All the same, many find it hard to pin down. For some, it's a dormitory suburb; some cite the traditional preponderance of pensioners while others resort to vague charges such as boredom and conformity. While not even Kungsholmen's own residents find characterisation easy, it's clear that the island has an unjust reputation.

This lack of identity has an historical explanation. Kungsholmen used to be a working-class area but without the cachet of other similar areas. Since the 17th century, when the city's foul-smelling tanneries were banished to Kungsholmen, all the heaviest and most polluting industries were located here. Life was primitive, with little to counterbalance the bleakness. At the turn of the 20th century, living conditions were so drastic the area was being called Starvation Island. Not even extensive housing devolpment in the thirties close behind the Central Station, nor the splendid residences by the water west of the City Hall helped foster real local pride.

A certain straightening of the back – and stiffening of the upper lip – has occurred only in the last two decades. Kungsholmen has come to be one of the 'in' places to live and a swarm of trendy restaurants and boutiques has opened. Some of the buildings along the waterside are numbered among Stockholm's most attractive addresses.

While there are still many valuable historical buildings

on the island, it's ironic that the most publicised preservation effort in recent years centred on an illuminated advertisement for Tulo throat lozenges dropping brightly down the side of a tall building. When the company balked at the sizable bill of 200,000 kronor for repairs, the city council chipped in.

Although the Old Town is often also called the Town between the Bridges, the title should rightfully belong to Kungsholmen, since no fewer than 12 bridges connect the island to the rest of the world, from the tiny Blekholmsbron footbridge to the majestic Västerbron. All in all, Kungsholmen has more bridges than any other area.

Living close to the water has always been important for Kungsholmers; water makes the island's periphery walk Stockholm's longest and arguably most delightful continuous waterside walkway. On the walk, you pass small swimming areas, boating and canoeing clubs and waterside cafés. It's a ten-kilometre stroll, taking non-athletes a couple of hours. Many do jog the distance, however, and some claim it is the world's most beautiful inner-city track.

From the air, two features stand out: one is the sharp division between east and west. The east is dominated by tight ranks of apartment blocks while the west is chiefly offices, factories and storage depots. On the east side is the City Hall, the most obvious symbol of municipal power. Within a radius of 500 metres are virtually all of the key municipal and county government, police

headquarters and the County Court. The other feature is the vivisection of the western side by traffic. Major roads cut deep, ugly slashes in the cityscape. Almost 200,000 vehicles transit western Kungsholmen every day.

The growling freeways have helped create a number of mini-neighbourhoods on western Kungsholmen. The people in these places tend to identify themselves as being from these neighbourhoods rather than from Kungsholmen proper.

And Kungsholmen's reputation as an oldies' ghetto? There is a grain of truth in this. Some parts are still pensioners' territories, but of a population of 53,000, 16 percent are 65 and older, which is about the same as in any other part of Stockholm. And Kungsholmen has more single-occupant dwellings than anywhere else in Stockholm – 70 percent of the residents are single. The mean age has dropped, however, and continues downward.

It is interesting, too, that nearly a third are immigrants, either foreign nationals or naturalised Swedes. This quotient is more than twice that of any other inner city area and is inceasingly reflected in commercial life.

Something else sets Kungsholmen apart: in other areas, people will often say they wouldn't dream of moving. But Kungsholmen knows no closed doors – residents identify themselves primarily as Stockholmers and many say they would have nothing against resettling elsewhere.

Perhaps Kungsholmen has the city's true cosmopolitans.

The City Hall viewing platform (p. 54).

City Hall, built with eight million bricks, is Kungsholmen's tallest building. To the right are typical thirties functionalistic apartment buildings. The rest of the buildings are from the decades either side of the turn of the nineteenth century (pp. 56–57).

A young Kungsholmer spends time in his own world (p. 58).

The stately Saint Erikspalatset and the Sportspalatset create a grand gateway to Kungsholmen. Saint Erikspalatset (foreground) was built in 1910, inspired by American skyscrapers. Sportspalatset opened in 1930, boasting Stockholm's first 50-metre swimming pool (p. 61).

The wide green swath of Rålambshov Park is alive with different games and activities in summer. Here free public gymnastics gathers the fit and the soon-to-be fit (p. 62).

A statue by Carl Eldh by the City Hall in perpetual pirouette as dusk falls (pp. 64–65).

Västerbro Bridge is probably the city's best-loved (left).

Stockholm City Hall, with its three burnished golden crowns has its inspiration in Venetian architecture. The 106-metre-high lookout tower gives an unrivalled view of the city (pp. 68–69).

CITY ON WATER

Had it not been for the water, Stockholm would not exist.
Defence and commerce needed easy access to water. Today's Stockholmers need water for other reasons – it's
impossible to imagine the capital without Riddarfjärden,
Strömmen and the many canals. Water frames the city and
provides its special character.

Stockholm is largely built on islands. About 30 bridges connect the islands with each other and the mainland. The quays are packed with thousands of ships and boats. Water is never distant and Stockholmers throng to it. They sail, fish, jog by the waterside or just stroll along the 16 kilometres of quayside. Water means freedom and open space, even for mere landlubbers.

But the water has had to make way for people. Several waterlands, lakes, inlets and ponds have disappeared over the centuries. What was once a fine body of water behind the main rail switching yard is now cement-lined canal. At the end of the 17th century, Stockholm had Europe's longest bridge: an 800-metre-long wooden construction. The bridge there now is only 80 metres long because land has been built on, displacing the water.

On the other hand, Stockholm's water is cleaner than for many years. Forty years ago, it was a polluted port. Today, you can swim in the city centre. In the summer, bathers can be seen enjoying the waters between moored boats along the quays of Lake Mälaren. You can also fish the year round in the rapids by the royal palace – the biggest recorded catch there is a 20 kilo salmon and there are few better places in the country to fish salmon trout. Successful trials have been going on for some years to get freshwater crayfish to settle in.

Stockholmers love their boats. There are several thousands of them at clubs and marinas around the Stockholm area – there are more than 30 boat clubs in the inner city. In summer, Riddarfjärden can be thick with white sail on a sunny Saturday, with races or regattas almost every weekend. Many will take the boat out in the evening after work. Along the quays, there's always activity around the boats. Canoeing has become popular and canoes or kayaks can be rented by the day or by the hour at several places. Some hardy souls paddle their kayaks to work and the vicious currents at Strömmen provide a welcome challenge for the best kayak paddlers almost year-round.

Along what is ironically called "The Quay of Dreams" at Strandvägen, and even at Söder and Norr Mälarstrand, on either side of Riddarfjärden, boats and schooners are tightly packed into the available space. All are in some stage of preparation for that trip to the Mediterranean or the West Indies. Many will never get beyond the scraping, painting, fixing and repairing while others, after ten years or so of backbreaking work, finally cast off for the voyage of a lifetime.

The city's waters aren't the exclusive domain of off-duty Stockholmers. Even if maritime traffic is far from what it was a hundred years ago, there is still a steady coming-and-going in the harbour. Every year, the habour berths 5,000 boats. Even though this is only a tenth of the volume of traffic in 1920, double the cargo tonnage of that year is moved through Stockholm yearly. There's still life in sea transport.

The Finland and Baltic ferry run is the busiest route by far: the world's biggest car ferries carry six million passengers back and forth every year. Worth noting is that one of Sweden's shortest ferry routes – from the Old Town to the Djurgården Park island – carries nearly two million passengers yearly. Tall masters or sailing schooners from foriegn ports always arouse attention in the harbour and cruise ships are regular visitors in the summer season.

Now that the maritime cargo business has diminished so much, many parts of the harbour have been turned into housing projects. Several boatyards have been forced to close, although the oldest of them all, on the old prison island of Långholmen, is still fully operational. It has been building ships on the same site for more than six centuries. Another, on Beckholmen islet, is still reparing everything from sailing-boats to archipelago steamers and ships.

Perhaps the archipelago ferries and steamers are dearest to the people's hearts. No other northern European city has so many steam-driven boats in working order – and in use. From spring to autumn, they are ferries, entertainment venues, restaurants and even wedding chapels. The smell of their hot engine oil and the glow of burnished brass on an autumn outing! When the archipelago steamers whistle, it's sweet music to Stockholmers.

Genuine, Stockholm-style water music.

A regatta on the waters of Riddarfjärden (p. 70).

Liljeholm Bridge is actually two bridges. The first was built in 1928 and the other in 1954 (pp. 72–73).

As the minesweeper HMS Visborg glides into Nybroviken Bay, a ship's cook suddenly emerges from a porthole to juggle oranges (p. 74).

These vessels along Söder Mälarstrand are used as homes, restaurants and offices (p. 77).

No other northern European city has so many steamboats. They're best viewed on Archipelago Boat Day (p. 78).

The choicest vantage point for city fireworks displays is on board a boat, close by. To the left is the Stadsgården quay and to the right, Beckholmen Island (pp. 80–81).

The harbour authorities can regulate the water level in Lake Mälaren. When they open the locks at Norrström, kayak sailors are estatic (left).

The waters of Norrström have both salmon and salmon trout (pp. 84–85).

Moored off the Vasa Museum are the icebreaker *St. Erik* and the lightship *Finngrundet* (pp. 86–87).

VASASTAN

Vasastan is more citified than other areas. No attempt has been made to make it a picturesque toytown; there are no sweeping parks or trendy pedestrian malls. Apartment buildings are wedged together and the streets are packed with people and cars. Small shops proliferate but parking spaces don't. Vasastan is the most densely populated city area, with few offices and no unpleasant administrative buildings nor ugly factories.

Vasastan is simply for living.

Vasastan is the most densely populated city area; 54,000 people live here, sharing 3.4 square kilometres. Street life reflects this, and Vasastan's pavements are crawling with people, especially youngsters. Except for Söder, the South Mount, no other area has such a high proportion of children.

The many professional people with solid incomes have obviously created a healthy commercial climate; a cornucopia of boutiques and restaurants characterises Vasastan. There are all of 250 small shops, offering everything from doll repairs to buttons. There are more antique shops than in any other area: 38 shops sell antiques or bric-a-brac.

Restaurant density is among the highest in Stockholm, with a couple of hundred eating places. Rörstrandsgatan is one of the best known restaurant streets in town.

An unlucky few know Vasastan only by what they see as they commute along several of the city's larger arteries. Had they the time or the inclination, they might delight in some of the area's out-of-the-way neighbourhoods, with names such as Turn of the Sun, Red Hills, Three Lilies and Atlas. All are small, semi-self-contained groups of apartment buildings. In these places, the city adopts another rhythm, street life is cosier and the architecture often creates a distinguishable skyline. Should one of those commuters by chance take a wrong turn, perhaps looking for a short cut, he might for a moment believe that he had strayed into a different city altogether. There's a feeling that city planners might have temporarily surrendered control.

The impression is reinforced from the air; Vasastan's streets reject the staid grid patterns of the other areas.

Karlbergsvägen, the main drag, crosses streets at haphazard angles. Another main thoroughfare, Odengatan, converges with it to form an improbably triangular 'square' at Odenplan. Nor are straight lines particularly common: no fewer than 14 streets in Vasastan are curved or dog-legged and there are four circular junctions. Several buildings allow passage through pleasingly shaped arches – urban echo chambers.

Vasastan has not had its name for very long. The name began to appear on maps in the 1920s. The Vasas were a royal dynasty, the first to rule over a united Sweden. Vasastan, meaning Vasa Town, was named after one of the main downtown streets, Vasagatan. Ironically, Vasagatan does not reach as far as Vasastan, although it does travel in the general direction.

It's a young area; 150 years ago, it was mostly forest and countryside, with occasional farms and idyllic glades. In the construction boom of the 1880s, Stockholm pushed outwards and upwards. Apartment blocks grew, resembling crude housing barracks, overcrowded from the start. Families, or extended families, often sharing a single room with adjoining kitchen. These 'single room' flats housed an average of four persons. By 1930, most of Vasastan had

been built and a quarter of the city's 400,000 people lived in the area.

Most of the buildings date from the same era, providing some architectural harmony. There's a dearth of ugly architecture and many of the older buildings have been renovated, especially in the 1970s and 1980s. Crowded living has been succeeded by interior roominess, with an average of two rooms per person. Some of the old courtyard structures have been razed, but Vasastan is largely as it was built, more than can be said for the other main city areas.

Vasastan is something of a frontier region. The neon-draped buildings by the old northern customs gate, Norrtull, tell travellers from the north that they are leaving the countryside and entering town; by the site of the old customs gate at Roslagstull, imposing apartment blocks give the feel of a city wall.

Nearby, Rörstrandsgatan steepens upwards and curves north. Beyond are rail tracks and the 'spaghetti junction' of the freeway, making it seem like a frontier outpost.

This is as far as the city goes.

The street of Gävlegatan epitomises the era of stone architecture (p. 88).

Perched on Observatory Hill is the old astronomic observatory. Since 1756, staff in the building have also taken weather readings several times a day, creating the world's longest unbroken meteorological record (pp. 90–91).

The City Library, designed by Gunnar Asplund, opened in 1928 (p. 92).

Vasastan is the city's most densely populated area. Courtyards are often ringed by double rows of apartment houses (p. 95).

Sveavägen is one of the city's busiest streets, with 50,000 vehicles passing through daily. Early in the morning, the rush has yet to begin (p. 96).

Children have played on Vasa Park's classic truck since the 1940s (pp. 98–99).

Seen from the southwest, Vasastan sprawls south, its main streets green ravines in the cityscape (right).

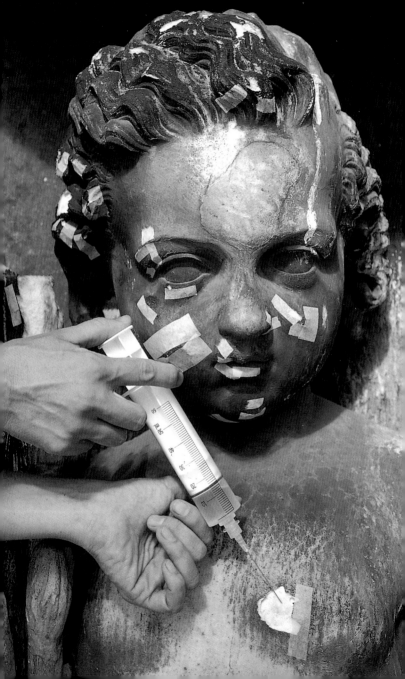

NORRMALM

This is the city's most contradictory area. The government, ministries and finance mix in with parks, quays and archipelago ferries. Norrmalm has the ugliest streets but also exquisite 17th century architecture. Few Stockholmers live in Norrmalm; many more spend their nine-to-fives here.

Sweden's power resides in Norrmalm. Government is headquartered a stone's throw from parliament. Every ministry and 50 civil departments are here. Riksbanken, the Central Bank, is ensconced on the highest spot, with the biggest banks all within a few hundred metres. Forty or more of Sweden's most powerful companies have their head offices here and innumerable foreign companies are represented.

Undeniably impressive. But making room for all these seats of power has been possible only through the most violent city planning. No other area has been so dramatically transformed. If all the rock blasted out during the 20th century went to make an island in the lake, there would be room enough on it for a whole extra neighbourhood. Hundreds of buildings have been razed and entire streets have been wiped from the map.

Huge office complexes have been erected on top of this battlefield of bedrock, using the most lifeless architecture imaginable. Parts of the central business district could be from any of Europe's many moribund banking districts. The difference is that neutral Sweden was not bombed in the Second World War – the damage done was the work of the city fathers.

The rebuilt downtown area, stripped of residential housing, became a ghost town at the end of the working day. In the vacuum, the disenfranchised of the city found leeway for drug dealing, prostitution and minor crimes of violence. This did not endear the downtown area to ordinary Stockholmers.

Luckily, Norrmalm has more than sterile office blocks and the smell of cement. The small, central Kungsträdgården Park is surrounded by restaurants and cafés and hums with life whatever the season. Another oasis is the immediate neighbourhood of Johannes Church, perched high above the hubbub of Sveavägen.

And in the quaint courtyard by the indoor swimming baths at Centralbadet, a turn-of-the-century atmosphere survives. Away by the Grand Hôtel, archipelago ferries whistle and toot as they cast off.

Much of Stockholm's entertainment is squeezed in here. Almost all the cinemas, hundreds of restaurants, bars and cafés as well as boundless shopping opportunities. There's music, too: the Royal Opera, the Concert Hall and the Academy of Music.

Unlike most cities, Stockholm has no main street. It's true that Kungsgatan, blasted from rock at the beginning of the 20th century, has always aspired to that title, but even if that street is still a fancy business address, it has never really fitted the part. Neither, for that matter, has any other contender.

Some streets are classier than others for doing business. Location, as always, is important if you're trying to attract shoppers. On an ordinary Saturday morning, over half a million people will flock downtown to do their shopping

or just window-shop. On any end-of-the-month Saturday, when salaries have just been paid, Norrmalm's shops will turn over about $15 million in a few short hours.

It has taken almost a generation for the downtown area to recover from the atrocities committed by planners and politicians in the 1960s. Among the newer attractions are the Stockholm City Theatre, housed in what used to be a makeshift parliament house. Two squares have been charmingly revamped – the traditional meeting place at Stureplan has been given a new lease of life following the re-routing of traffic, and Normalmstorg is now a piazza as lively as any in the world. But best of all, people are moving back to live in the downtown area. Six thousand now call Norrmalm home. The central business district itself had some years ago 1,000 inhabitants, but their number has been raised, with one or two elegant residential apartment buildings appearing at the end of the 20th century, right in the most needful areas. After more than two decades as Cement City, Stockholm's heart is slowly returning to life.

Stockholmers are reclaiming the downtown core, planting the flag once again in their own centre. Giving it life again.

A careful renovation for the sculptures on the National-museum facade (p. 102).

The gigantic royal finger of the warrior king, Karl XII, who is a statue in Kungsträdgården Park (p. 104–105).

The black granite of the Central Bank dominates its sur-roundings. Architect Peter Celsing wanted the building to look like a treasure chest, although whether money is kept here is a closely guarded secret (p. 106).

Only a minute from the noisy Sergels Torg Square is the tranquillity of Johannes Church. The traditional wooden clock tower from 1692 is far older than the church itself, consecrated in 1890 (p. 108).

Klaraberg Street is a rush hour hub, with commuter trains, buses and the metro transport system (p. 110).

The ellipsoid glass fountain at Sergels Torg Square. The lights of the fountain blaze dimly against those of the city centre (pp. 112–113).

Rain temporarily spoils the otherwise hectic café-life in Kungsträdgården Park (left).

Per-Olof Borin has brightened up the public pavement out-side his downtown apartment. Watering flowers takes time, since pedestrians will often stop to chat (pp. 116–117).

Stockholm's property owners are traditionally conscien-tious about the decorative features of their buildings. Anders Hellberg gives an aluminium spire a fresh coat of paint (pp. 118–119).

A tranquil morning by Norrmalm's Nybroviken Bay, which got its current form in the beginning of the 1900s. A hun-dred and fifty years back the water reached further inland with the present park still part of the inlet (right).

The angel Victoria, sculpted by Aron Sandberg, stands atop one of the twin towers that overlook Kungsgatan. Her horn serves to remind passersby that the building was erected by the Ericsson Telephone Company (p. 122).

The horses of Blasieholmen Square attract many young riders. The horses are modelled on Byzantine originals on the roof of the Marcus Basilica in Venice (p. 123).

Hötorget has been a market square since the 1600s and is the best – and most fun – place in Stockholm to buy fruit and vegetables. Most stalls are manned by immigrants who maintain the square's lively commercial traditions (pp. 124–125).

Just outside the very heart of the city, the facades facing the street of Strömgatan evoke earlier days. Fishermen have used similar bag nets in this stretch of water since the Middle Ages (left).

ÖSTERMALM

The boulevard system promotes neatness. Straight streets, well maintained facades and trimmed parks. Östermalm is a new area, created just a hundred years ago to demonstrate Stockholm's coming of age as a city. At first, it was an enclave for the prosperous, and the reputation has stuck. But Östermalm is far more than a haven for aristocrats and millionaires.

Stockholm's newest area was in the throes of construction when writer August Strindberg noted: "We clear the way for light and air." The shantytown that had occupied the area was being razed to the ground. New buildings were being erected along neat, symmetrically planned streets; grandiose boulevards stretched the length of the area and to top it all off, it was renamed. The old name, Ladugårdslandet, Barnfields, proved far too rustic a name for the proud new inhabitants. Östermalm, or East Mount, was more fittingly neutral. Quickly, the spacious new apartment buildings were filled with senior civil servants, artistocrats, military officers and others of the upper crust, attracted by the new area's stylish atmosphere.

Stockholm never quite succeeded in joining the ranks of the truly swank European cities; not even the brand new district helped. Perhaps the countryside was still too close at hand, perhaps Stockholmers were at heart too down-to-earth; the small town feeling simply would not disappear on command. Not even the boulevards really worked well. In contrast to Paris, where huge boulevards depart from some magnificent place and arrive at a huge stone arch, the boulevards of Stockholm have neither beginning nor end. One of the most impressive, Strandvägen, is born in a chaotic roundabout and fades out in a weak bend. Karlavägen, another fine, wide street, begins abruptly and ends in ... nothing. Yet another, Narvavägen, has lent its median space to parking and become one of Stockholm's largest car parks.

The area has its share of small, hidden streets with three-storey buildings and, a rarity in urban Sweden, private gardens. It's a truly verdant area, not only in the generous space of Huumlegården Park and the elongated Gustav Adolf Park, but also in the smaller, lesser known parks. There are more than 70 embassies and consulates in Östermalm, giving it a strongly international feel.

There is also the distinctly continental market hall, preserved as the last of the old food emporiums, with its meat and game and mounds of fresh fruit and vegetables.

Östermalm's grandest detail may be the interior height of its ceilings. This can be seen from the street; a five-storey building in Östermalm is frequently taller than a five-storey anywhere else. Apartments are larger here than elsewhere in Stockholm. For example, there are more than two thousand apartments of seven rooms or more – four times the number of any other area. For the area's 55,000 inhabitants compact living will always be an abstract concept. And all the aristocrats and millionaires? In fact, although mean income is not vastly higher than in other areas, there is an abundance of millionaires. And Östermalm is home to more than 300 counts and barons.

You would not say that Östermalm's strong suit is change and renewal; the tendency is more towards preservation and maintenance of what seems to work well. When, in the 1980s, drug addicts began using Stockholm's classic water fountains to rinse syringes, the city fathers simply turned

off the water – everywhere, that is, except on Karlaplan Place; the fountain there was beautiful and functional and Östermalmers were not about to let junkies pressure them. The fountain still quenches the thirst of the parched pedestrians.

Neither is the architecture much changed. The postwar craze for renewal made few inroads in conservative Östermalm. One of the few, drastic changes is the behemoth of Garnisonen – at the time of construction, northern Europe's largest office complex. Close on its heels come the Swedish Radio Company's headquarters.

Paradoxically, the area with the straightest street grid is difficult to negotiate by car. In their zeal to maintain the tranquillity of Östermalm, the city fathers produced traffic restrictions so harsh that even the most experienced of Stockholm's motorists can get stuck. It's best negotiated on foot. Walking will give you time to discover all the subtleties and excitement: intricate details of house facades, tiny art galleries, hidden streets and all the friendly people. Recommended: a slow gait and alert eyes.

It's called strolling. Östermalm is the home of the stroll.

Karlaplan Square is the hub for Östermalm's broad esplanades (p. 128).

Children are well catered for in Östermalm. A feminist figurehead, Fredrika Bremer, looks after schoolbags while children play in Humlegården Park (p. 130).

The dials of Oscar's Church mimic the bright moon (p. 133).

The Garnisonen office complex is one of Östermalm's least typical structures. The area is made up mostly of attractive buildings in stone. (p. 134).

Home-made speedsters make use of a smoother slope (pp. 136–137).

"Tradesmen Kindly Use the Kitchen Entrance at No. 62," says this brass sign. Östermalm makes no effort to hide its blue-blooded past (left).

The Sturebadet health club complex is a copy of the original baths, built at the beginning of the 20th century and destroyed by fire in 1985 (pp. 140–141).

To check the stability of the cross above Engelbrekt Church, Rolf Carlsson shakes and tugs it as hard as he can (right).

Strandvägen was created partly by landfill at the end of the 19th century to be the city's showpiece street. The first residents were the city's economic upper crust. All the spires and domes were perhaps intended to heighten the palatial atmosphere. (pp. 144–145).

Östermalm's market hall, built in 1889, is one of the city's grandest girded constructions. Produce from imported foie gras to the lowly potato is on offer (left).

THE URBAN NATIONAL PARK

Stockholm has countryside literally within minutes of downtown – open fields and thick forest. Stockholmers have been picnicking, partying, hiking and walking in forest and field for centuries. Now, it's in writing: a swath of trees and fields in the city has been designated the world's first urban national park.

Numerous poets and writers – some more expert than others – have sung the praises of the city's lush surroundings, where generations have flocked for relief from the aches and pains of city life. There are hidden corners of special beauty and charm but what is most special is the unity of Stockholm's parkland, that so close to the centre of a capital city of Stockholm's size there is an impressive acreage of hills and pastures, parks and forests, still largely undeveloped. The buildings in the parklands are often unusual: gazebos, antique timber houses, romantic villas, 30 museums and three royal palaces, Ulriksdal, Haga and Rosendal.

The city is beating at the door, however, and precious parkland has already been surrendered to huge gas cisterns, a harbour for oil tankers and Stockholm's highest structure, the Kaknäs communication tower.

Which is why a government decree in 1994 made the entire green belt into an urban national park – the world's first. The park stretches in a ragged crescent from some of the islands in the heart of the city to the great Djurgården Park, past the university, taking in the magnificent 'English Park' at Haga, and beyond to another royal property, the stately palace grounds of Ulriksdal.

In the words of the law: "Within the confines of an urban national park, buildings may be raised and construction undertaken only if this can be accomplished without disruption of the character of the park or natural environment and without damage to the natural and historical characteristics of the landscape." In other words, look but please don't touch.

Despite its immediate proximity to Sweden's busiest places, the park area has been well maintained. The main reason is that even though the park is state-owned, much of it has been under the monarch's personal protection for centuries. A large section was originally used for cattle grazing or mixed farming, and later for the royal hunt. There was farming in the area up until the middle of the 20th century and a flock of sheep, famed as "the King's sheep" is still brought to graze on a field in the park each summer.

Since the 18th century, however, the park belt has been the city's green lungs, an extensive parkland for picnics and festivals or just ambling in. There has been serious partying in the park, too – so riotous in the 19th century that restrictions were imposed on the use of alcohol in public parks. The serving of alcohol in park restaurants after midnight was made conditional on special permission from the royal Office of the Governor of Stockholm; the governor had to be convinced that alcohol was "necessary for the conviviality of the occasion".

An estimated 15 million visitors visit the urban national park each year. Many come to see Skansen, the spacious outdoor museum of cultural history, or the amusement park at Gröna Lund or the many other museums. Others are there for events such as organised amateur cycle races,

the kite festival or the many outdoor concerts in the grounds of the Maritime Museum. Most of them simply need to be close to nature – ideally within bus range of the centre.

More of the urban park is cared for than is left wild but there are several considerable areas of forest. There are 800 wildflower species. A hundred species of nesting birds and deer are often seen. Djurgården Park itself has one of Europe's best forests of giant oak; 50 or more measure at least five metres around the trunk. The oaks, in turn, are home to nothern Europe's densest population of tawny owls.

Its status as urban national park is important protection for the area but Stockholmers will continue to use their favourite few haunts, blissfully ignorant of the green area's new pedigree. Long before there was such a thing as an urban national park, all this was deeply embedded in the hearts of Stockholmers.

A bicycle enveloped by greenery on the street of Långa gatan (p. 148).

A marsh called Isbladskärret is Sweden's most accessible bird preserve. Only a few steps off a popular promenade through the Djurgården Park is a sizeable colony of heron (pp. 150–151).

Although the Baroque-style park at the royal property of Ulriksdal is one of the country's most beautiful, few Stockholmers find their way here (p. 152).

The magnificent grassy slope in Haga Park is called the Great Pelouse (p. 155).

By 1834, it had taken nine years to dredge the Djurgårdsbrunn Canal. It had been used by seacraft years earlier but as the land rose, it became impassable. Dredging was funded by tolls, with barges paying most. Today, passage is free and barge traffic is only a memory (p. 157).

The flag has been raised at Kastellholmen Islet since 1640. One legend has it that, should the ceremony be neglected, the country would be in danger of invasion (pp. 158–159).

Kaknäs Tower, 161 metres high, is Stockholm's tallest structure (left).

Dawn on Gärdet Common, on the eastern side of the city. This is paradise for city dogs; leash restrictions do not apply here and there's lots of canine company (pp. 162–163).

The sheep that graze every summer in fields in northern Djurgården Park may belong to Johan Gustafsson, but Stockholmers still call them "the Kings sheep", because of an old royal privilege (pp. 164–165).

The warship *Vasa* is the world's only preserved 17th century ship. The fiasco of the ship's capsize minutes into its maiden voyage in 1628 has turned to triumph; the ship is now one of the world's top museum attractions. After having been lost and forgotten for centuries, the *Vasa* was found by a stubborn researcher in the 1950s and salvaged virtually intact in 1961 (right).

The two innermost archipelago islands, Kastellholmen and Skeppsholmen, are right in the city – and also the most central sections of the urban national park (pp. 168–169).

In Sweden's northernmost beech forest, at Liston Hill, the scratchings in the bark reveals stories of lovers (pp. 170–171).

A hundred bird species nest in Stockholm's urban national park. A broken jetty lantern is perfect for a broody gull (left).

Ever since Gustav III had a landscape architect design Haga Park in the 1700s, it's been a favourite picnic place for Stockholmers. In the early morning, though, you might almost have the park to yourself (pp. 174–175).

ANOTHER YEAR

Stockholm doesn't have just one pulse – it has several.
There's the rhythm of the sailboats and the rhythm of
the helicopters. The courier bikes use one gear and the
rubbish collectors another. But there's a deeper rhythm,
attuned to the seasons. There are many ways to experi-
ence the city's beat.

The ice of Årstaviken Inlet has captured a remembrance of summer, framing the extremes of the Stockholm year (p. 176).

The snow-covered rooftops of the Old Town, viewed from the German Church, seem adrift in time, close as they are to the commercial centre (pp. 178–179).

The biting cold of January has already spread thick ice on Riddarfjärden, giving citizens a new promenade (pp. 180–181).

Two curious dogs on Kastellholmen Islet nose out the steam coming off the water (left).

Ice yachts reach speeds of 70 kilometres per hour close to the city (pp. 184–185).

Hardy souls have been taking winter dips on Kungsholmen since the 1920s (left).

Winter birds gravitate to the ice-free waters where the lake drops into the sea (pp. 188–189).

Walpurgis night at Tantolunden (pp. 190–191).

Encouched in lilacs, a typical old Söder house. To the left can be seen the tower of what was once a factory owner's home. Further to the left is the water of Riddar-fjärden (pp. 192–193).

At the Skansen open air museum, maypoles have been circled since 1891. Skansen attracts some 25,000 people every Midsummer Eve (left).

Hot days turn Stockholmers into sea creatures. Teenagers show their daring by diving from the support of Västerbro Bridge while others bathe at Långholmen Island or Smeds-udden (pp. 196–197).

Even in the city there's the rustic magic of the forests. On a late August evening, a couple dallies among water-lilies, scarcely thinking of the thick mud at their feet (p. 198–199).

With the coming autumn, the air becomes damp. A bank of fog sweeps in from the lake, soon to cover the city (left).

In Haga Park, shadows lengthen inexorably (pp. 202–203).

Many Stockholmers long for the clear, brisk days of autumn. But sometimes reality doesn't measure up (pp. 204–205).

The first snow is always a surprise. Residents stroll along Norr Mälarstrand, uncertain whether the season change is for real (pp. 206–207).

Candles are lit in Skogskyrkogården Cemetery on All Souls' Day. This is the city's biggest cemetery with over a hundred thousand graves (pp. 208–209).

Stockholm in winter seen through a telephoto lens makes close neighbours of normally widely dispersed landmarks (left).

The first Nobel Prize banquet was held in the Grand Hôtel in 1901. Since 1926, the venue has been the cavernous Blue Hall at the City Hall (pp. 212–213).

Bad weather strikes suddenly. A postman struggles against the snow and minimal visibility (left).

It's the mid-December St. Lucia morning ritual in Gustav Vasa Church. Children from the Adolf Fredrik Music School fill the almost hundred-year-old church with traditional St. Lucia and Christmas songs (pp. 216–217).

Christmas in Stockholm begins with a bang – on 23 December, the Queen's birthday brings a 21-gun salute (pp. 218–219).

INDEX

This is a compact edition of *Stockholm Horizons*, the acclaimed photographic book about the Swedish capital. The original format was 24 x 33 cm, ISBN 91-89204-11-5. Both compact and classic editions are published in Swedish as *Staden*, ISBN 91-89204-60-3 (compact) and ISBN 91-89204-10-7 (classic).